CRYPTOCURRENCY EXPLAINED

CRYPTOCURRENCY

BEGINNERS BIBLE

CRYPTOCURRENCY EXPLAINED Copyright

© 2010 by B.Winder

All rights reserved. This book or any portion thereof
may not be reproduced or used in any manner whatsoever
without the express written permission of the publisher
except for the use of brief quotations in a book review.

Table of Contents

Cryptocurrency: 1

The Fundamental Guide to Cryptocurrency Investing For Beginner's. .... Error! Bookmark not defined.

Introduction 4

Chapter 1 : The History Of Cryptocurrency 7

Chapter 2: Cryptocurrency Vs. Fiat Currency 9

Chapter 3: Other Ways To Make Money With Bitcoin 19

Chapter 4: Benefits And Risks Of Investing 30
    Benefits 30
    Risks 34

Chapter 5: Tips For Trading 43

Chapter 6: The Most Common Cryptocurrencies 58

Chapter 7: Cryptocurrency Exchanges 69

Chapter 8: The Future Of Cryptocurrency 86

Conclusion 91

Introduction

Cryptocurrencies are basicly virtual money used within a computer system. They are a series of digital records held by multiple parties, which track the amount of currency that individual wallets hold. A cryptocurrency can be said to be an asset which has been digitally designed to function as a medium of exchange. Cryptocurrencies uses cryptography to protect and enhance transactions and to manage the inclusion of more units of that particular currency. Widely considered as alternatives to real currencies, cryptocurrencies are commonly referred to as digital currencies.

Matthew Field and Cara McGoogan, correspondents from the British newspaper The Telegraph, said that cryptocurrencies are types of private, virtual money intended to be adequately protected at all times. Cryptocurrencies are linked to the net and created using cryptographic processes. Their creation also involves the conversion of information into codes that are very difficult to crack, which essentially monitor their exchanges throughout the network.

Field and McGoogan said that originally, cryptographic procedures developed out of the need to protect the transmission of news and information during World War II. In the modern digital world, it metamorphosed into the foundation for the online distribution of private and protected information, with the help of advanced knowledge in computer science and more complex mathematical calculations.

Cryptocurrencies are usually referred to as "digital gold" because through preservation, they increase in value over time. As a medium of payment, cryptocurrencies are easy and convenient to use around the globe. Because transactions using cryptocurrencies are generally transparent, they also operate as a medium of payment in illegal transactions or activities.

Cryptocurrencies have given a massive kickstart to a new and rapidly growing marketplace. For instance, Poloniex (an exchange platform) has assisted in the trading of countless cryptocurrencies since they surfaced. Many of these exchange platforms experience larger percentages of trades than some European stock exchanges.

Chapter 1 : The History Of Cryptocurrency

In 1998 Wei Dai a computer engineer, published an article that described a possible new form of currency. He called it "b-money." He further explained that it would be an anonymous, distributed electronic cash system. It was only a few steps away from how much money is handled and used for paying things online.

Eager to take advantage of this idea, Nick Szabo, a computer scientist and legal scholar, created "bit gold." This was the first prototype of the first real, decentralized cryptocurrency and the one that produced a workable system was Bitcoin; created by Satoshi Nakamoto. Bitcoin uses a system known as SHA-256, a set of hash functions that were actually designed by the United States' National Security Agency. SHA-256 ensures proof of work so that cryptocurrency is reliable.

"Proof of work" - This is a system that prevents scamming and fraud. It requires some proof of work from the person requesting the service to prove that they are aboveboard. It also has to be easy enough for the service provider to regulate and check up on the work. Usually, this "proof of work" means processing time by a computer. In 2011, two years after Bitcoin unleashed the cryptocurrency market, Namecoin was created. Namecoin was made to form a decentralized DNS, which makes internet censorship more difficult. This means that governments can't monitor or control your cryptocurrency trading, buying, and spending. In the years since the creation of Bitcoin and Namecoin, other forms of "altcoin" were created—and we'll get to the definition of that in just a moment—but none of them have lasted very long because they haven't brought anything new to the table. Some forms of altcoins have been able to use modifications to further the market, such as Litecoin, which used script instead of SHA-256 to ensure regulation and credibility, but for the most part, Bitcoin has been the cryptocurrency that has reigned supreme.

Chapter 2: Cryptocurrency Vs. Fiat Currency

So how does cryptocurrency measure up against fiat currency? As always, when embarking on a project, understand that there are pros and cons. The key is to see if the pros outweigh the cons, not to find something that has no cons whatsoever. Keep in mind as you embark on your cryptocurrency adventure that if something sounds too good to be true, it usually is.

However, there are some distinct advantages that cryptocurrency has over fiat currency, especially if you are looking to trade and get into the cryptocurrency trading market.

Fiat currency, whether in cash or digital, is essentially the currency that is controlled and regulated by the government. It's the "official" money of that country, and you can't technically buy anything within that country unless you are using that currency. When buying something in another country using digital means such as a credit card, the computer will do the money converting for you. Taking, say, your US dollars and converting them into British pounds as the purchase is made. But if you only have cash, you need to go to a bank or somewhere else to get your dollars exchanged for the pounds so that you can then go out and make your purchases. Cryptocurrency, on the other hand, has no such government regulations and can be used in any country. This brings us to our first benefit in trading with cryptocurrency rather than fiat currency: inflation.

Inflation is where there is more cash money out in the world, and so it is less valuable as a result. The more of something there is, the less valuable it is. That means that your one dollar bill will buy you less because it has less value, and so suppliers are asking for more money to make up the difference. Consider the difference in pricing for a cup of coffee in the 1950s, which was ten cents, to today, which is up to six dollars. That is a huge rate of inflation, and it means that you can't rely on fiat money. While we haven't seen anything as major as the Great Depression in the 1930s, that doesn't mean that it can't in some way happen again. In 2008, the world saw another huge financial crisis that only narrowly avoided becoming as bad as the Great Depression. Part of this is because of the dependence on the fiat money. Large banks and money-focused companies such as investment banks—companies that have repeatedly proven that they are happy to sacrifice your dollars in favor of conducting schemes and fraud to increase the ludicrous lifestyles of their CEOs. This is a huge problem because there's no way of regulating just how much money is in circulation or how much money the government is printing.

In the cryptocurrency world, there is a cap on how many cryptocurrencies there are. Bitcoin, for example, has a cap of 21 million bitcoins. This created a "controlled supply," and because it is controlled and finite, its value is assured. The coins are designed to eventually go out of circulation as new ones are created, so that there is never more than the cap out in circulation. It means that there is constantly a decreasing supply of bitcoins, rather than an increasing supply. This was designed to mimic the way the gold community works, which is why the volunteers who ensure that everything is regulated are called "miners," since they are "mining" the "gold" aka the bitcoins. This ensures that there is no inflation and that the value of your cryptocurrency isn't going to suddenly collapse or go down. Unlike with fiat money, you have security. In fact, your bitcoin's value will increase over time, something that happens with metal and gemstones but never with fiat money.

Another big advantage that cryptocurrency has over fiat money is that you don't have to report it for taxes. Every year, people are forced to pay their government large sums of money, and often those who are paying the most are the ones who can least afford to. The rich get barely anything taken away while the poor have to hand over money when they're already struggling with bills. With cryptocurrency, you don't have to worry about anything that you own being taken away from you. Cryptocurrency is untaxed and you don't have to report it to the government tax agency unless you want to. Cryptocurrency recognizes your individual sovereignty, which means that what you do with your currency is up to you, not the government. However, fiat currency still holds a potentially large advantage over cryptocurrency and that is the issue of legality. Some governments absolutely forbid cryptocurrency while others try to regulate it, such as the United State. Depending on what country you're from, you might want to ensure that you're careful about the law, or at least familiar with the law in regards to cryptocurrency.

While this might be something that brings you up short about cryptocurrency, remember that the reason governments are having such a problem with it is that they can't regulate it. It's difficult to actually bring the law down on someone when you can't regulate and properly explain why what they were doing was wrong. Until governments come up with solid rules about cryptocurrency, they can't generally take people to task for using it. Of course, there are exceptions, but if you're getting busted by the government for using cryptocurrency, you were probably being busted in the cryptocurrency community as well. For example, thanks to the miners, it's virtually impossible to create your own bitcoins and use them to purchase things or to play with the market. You're caught almost immediately and can have all of your cryptocurrency confiscated or be kicked out of the community. When it comes to cryptocurrency, governments are mostly just gnashing their teeth in frustration. Until the governments of the world come up with solid rules about cryptocurrency, you shouldn't let the rather small fear of legality get in your way of taking advantage of this amazing opportunity. Cryptocurrency is viewed by most governments at this point as a nuisance, a buzzing fly, and they have so many other things to worry about that it's not exactly their top priority to take care of it.

Another advantage that cryptocurrency has is that it cannot be destroyed and it is always in your possession. A lost wallet means you have to call your bank, cancel your credit or debit card, and get a new one, and any cash that you had in there is permanently lost. If your cash gets wet, or catches on fire, or gets stained or torn... you get the picture. Cash can be destroyed or lost. Cryptocurrency can't. Furthermore, the banks and governments of the world actually have the right to destroy fiat currency since they are the ones who create and control it. Nobody can do that to your cryptocurrency, so your money is always safe.

Cryptocurrency also takes just minutes to transfer, which means that buying, selling, and trading can take place in half the time. Fiat currency has to pass through a bunch of regulations and checkpoints, so something as simple as transferring money from one person's account to another can take days—especially on weekends. Cryptocurrency transfers take minutes. You also don't have to pay a fee, whether it's from your bank or it's taxes or anything else, for transferring money. And you don't have to worry about the value of your money going up or down. An American traveling to Britain or an Australian traveling to America would suddenly find the value of their money going down. What would have cost them five dollars in their home country now costs them seven, or eight, or even ten dollars in their new country. With cryptocurrency, the market is international, and so the money's value is international. It stays the same no matter where you are or who you're buying from or what you're saying or when you're trading. You can have the assurance of your money's value.

All this adds up to the simple truth that you have control over your cryptocurrency. Not a bank or a government, but you. You know your cryptocurrency's value, and how much value it will have down the line. You know how much you're spending and don't have to worry about banks or the government taxing that money, taking it away, destroying it, or decreasing its value. You give and receive money quickly, within minutes. You actually have the power to control your finances rather than finding yourself at the mercy of institutions that don't care and aren't regulated and controlled the way that they should. Not to mention you don't have to report anything to anyone. Your bank is always in control of where you spend your money, and can stop a transfer of funds if it seems suspicious to them. You always have to be able to explain your funds and how you're spending them, and you don't have any privacy. With cryptocurrency, you don't have someone breathing down your neck that way. You have privacy and don't need to worry about having your account frozen because you bought a computer while vacationing in Europe.

Finally, the fact of the matter is that the dollar is dying. Already governments are struggling to figure out how they will move forward with currency in the future, whether to go cash-free, to create a new monetary system, and so on. While we like to think that our governments will eventually figure things out—and maybe they will—what it means for now is that investing in cryptocurrency will provide you with financial security that a dollar can't. While the rest of the world struggles to handle what to do with their dying economies, you can be assured of your assets and make sure that you are financially stable and taken care of through any financial crisis that may arise. This is especially true for those living in the United States. With the country's debt approaching $19 trillion and other nations doing their best to actually avoid using the U.S. dollar, it's only a matter of time before there's another collapse.

Cryptocurrency is dependable and on the rise, whereas fiat currency is declining. Getting in now and getting ahead will only benefit.

The result of cryptocurrency versus fiat currency? One is the future and the other is the past. Once you understand that, it's easy to know where you need to invest.

Chapter 3: Other Ways To Make Money With Bitcoin

Since bitcoin's recent highs, the cryptocurrency has once again awoken the interest of the media, regulators, and speculators.

Buying and Holding Bitcoins

If you want to start earning bitcoin you first need to obtain a bitcoin wallet, which is used to send, receive and store your bitcoins. You can obtain one from an online based service such as Coinbase or Blockchain.info. These are two of the most used bitcoin wallet and come with an online and a mobile version. Having said that, the safest way to store your bitcoins would be offline. For that, you could use a so-called "cold wallet" such as Trezor.

Once you have a wallet service, you can establish multiple bitcoin addresses, which allow you to receive bitcoins from others. No real life addresses are necessary, just your bitcoin address will suffice for any digital currency transfers. All transaction can then be viewed on the blockchain at Blockchain.info. This is why bitcoin is considered as a semi-anonymous digital currency as transactions are linked to bitcoin addresses but who is behind those addresses is unknown.

Bitcoin Mining

we love bitcoinMining bitcoins can be quite complex and is usually not recommended for beginners. The process entails the use of sophisticated machines that are expensive and consume quite a lot of electricity to solve mathematical algorithms in exchange for bitcoins. Bitcoin miners enable bitcoin transactions by sharing their processing power. In exchange for enabling the bitcoin network to function, they are rewarding with new bitcoins. This is what "mining" refers to.

Having said that, it is no longer considered lucrative for individuals to mine at home using mining equipment and the shift is being made towards more large-scale operations.

If you do want to engage in bitcoin mining and are willing to invest in expensive mining hardware, it is strongly advisable to join a mining pool. In a mining pool, miners pool their resources together and share their hashing power with the aim of solving a block and dividing the reward equally. It is an effective way to motivate small-scale miners to continue their involvement in mining activities. Some popular mining pools are:

—Antpool

—BTCC

—SlushPool

—Bitcoin Cloud Mining

Alternatively, you could engage in bitcoin cloud mining. Bitcoin cloud mining is the process of mining bitcoins using a remote datacenter with shared processing power. Cloud mining is beneficial to individuals as it allows them to carry out their mining activities without having to manage the mining hardware.

It enables you to earn bitcoins without mining software, mining hardware, bandwidth, electricity or other offline issues. However, there is a cost associated with cloud mining as a service and this will have an effect on your bottom line.

The most reputable cloud mining company is Genesis Mining. I personally have a small bitcoin mining contract running with them. Having said that, the time it will take you to break even on bitcoin cloud mining can easily take well over a year and that is assuming the price of bitcoin doesn't drop. If you want to play your part in the bitcoin network and want to mine at a low cost, then cloud mining is a good option. If you are looking for a lucrative investment, however, you are much better off just buying the cryptocurrency itself or engaging in peer-to-peer bitcoin lending.

Bitcoin Faucets

Bitcoin Faucet. If you who enjoy playing games or simply don't mind looking at a few ads, you can visit bitcoin faucet websites. These websites generate revenue from ads placed on their pages and pay out a small amount of the ad revenue to its users. All you need to do is sign up with your bitcoin address and start earning a few cents worth of bitcoin every day.

While it is a very slow way to earn bitcoins, these sites allow anyone new to bitcoin to get obtain bits of the crypto-currency for free.

Some of the most reputable and large faucets that have consistently made their payouts over a long time period include Moon Bitcoin, Bitcoin Aliens, and BTCclicks.

Completing Microtasks for Bitcoin

You can also earn bitcoins by completing micro-tasks on the following platforms:

Bituro is a smartphone app that pays you in bitcoins for small tasks, such as watching promotional videos, filling out surveys and testing apps.

Bitcoin Reward enables you to earn for watching videos, downloading and testing apps, filling out market research surveys and other minor tasks. Coinbucks is a smartphone app that allows you to earn bitcoins for playing mobile games, downloading smartphone apps and completing online promotional offers.

Day-Trading Bitcoin for a Profit

If you love the financial markets and regularly trade online then day-trading bitcoin could be a way for you to make money with bitcoin.

When it comes to bitcoin trading, the basic speculation strategy applies. You buy when the currency is low and wait for the price to increase before you sell it a higher price to generate profit. It is important you understand market trends and price dynamics if you want to make successful trades. Bitcoin is primarily headline driven, it is important to follow bitcoin news closely when actively trading the digital currency. Some exchanges also allow you to trade bitcoin using leverage, which can help you increase your trading profit but also possess a much higher downside risk.

Bitcoin chart

You can also trade in bitcoin via arbitrage; buy it cheap on one exchange and sell it at a higher price on another exchange.

Becoming a Market Marker on Localbitcoins.com

Localbitcoins.com allows you to trade Bitcoins for fiat currencies through individual trades, sometimes referred to as over the counter trading or OTC. Most people are comfortable selling bitcoins over the counter as the transactions are fast and they offer diverse methods of payment.

Hundreds of bitcoin traders from around the globe are making profits on Localbitcoins by becoming market makers (buying and selling in Localbitcoins). Here is a brief guide on how to sell bitcoins on LocalBitcoins.com.

1. First, you sign up to LocalBitcoins.com

2. Then, you need to create an online sell advertisement for bitcoins. When designing an advertisement you select a payment method, set you pricing limits and outline your terms of trade as a free-form message.

3. Next, you need to replenish your wallet with bitcoin, for you to order customers to be able to access trade requests from your advertisements.

Once a buyer opens a trade with you, the full bitcoin amount is automatically transferred from your wallet to escrow.

When the buyer has made the payment and pressed the Mark payment complete button you will receive an SMS alert or a notification via email informing you that payment of the trade has been done.

Upon confirmation of the payment, the bitcoins are released to the buyer from the escrow to his Localbitcoins wallet.

The last step is to leave feedback for the buyer so as to gain reputation and make some trades.

Depending on the country, bid/offer prices vary greatly. If you are making markets in less saturated bitcoin markets, you can make easy money as a market maker on LocalBitcoins.

Gambling in Online Bitcoin Casinos

Gambling. If you like gambling online and want to earn your gambling winnings in bitcoin, then you can choose from a variety of bitcoin casinos and gambling sites. Leading bitcoin online gambling sites include Starcoin, Crypto Games, BetKing, and vDice.

When you like playing dice, roulette, poker, lottery or slots, the bitcoin online gambling market is more than big enough to satisfy your gambling needs.

Investing in Bitcoin Peer-to-Peer Loans

You can also use your bitcoins to lend them to entrepreneurs and small SMEs using the bitcoin peer-to-peer lending platform Bitbond. You can generate excellent returns by lending through Bitbond.

Peer-to-peer lending refers to a method through which individuals, startups, and SMEs can borrow from individuals without the use of a traditional financial intermediary. This enables financing for those who are finding it hard to secure a loan from a bank and generates strong fixed interest returns, with low transaction fees and a low correlation to stocks and bonds for investors.

However, remember to always diversify your risk by lending to a number of borrowers as opposed to putting all your money into one loan.

Selling Goods and Services in Exchange for Bitcoin

Make Money With Bitcoin and finally, one of the most common ways of earning bitcoins is by selling goods or services in exchange for bitcoins. Some of the things you can sell are clothes, old gadgets, cars and even homes in exchange for bitcoin. Presently, there a lot of sites that offer platforms for people to buy and sell products in exchange for bitcoins.

Two popular sites to sell products in exchange for bitcoin are Bitify and Purse.

Bitify:

Bitify.com is somewhat likened to the Ebay for Bitcoin. It uses an auction system to sell items in exchange for bitcoins. Bitify also offers escrow services so that buyers can ensure the goods are delivered to them first before releasing the bitcoins. The use of the escrow service is optional for buyers at a 1% fee. Sellers, on the other hand, have a 2.5% fee on the total sale price of the items. Premium advertisements are charged at 1.5% of the total cost.

Purse.io:

Individuals with amazon accounts can sell items at a discount on Purse. Buyers who use bitcoin advertise their wish lists on at their Purse.io accounts.

Alternatively, you could sell services, as a freelancer for example, and get paid in bitcoin. There are many bitcoin-based freelancer platforms where one can offer their services, such as BitGigs or Coinality.

Chapter 4: Benefits And Risks Of Investing in Cryptocurrency

Benefits

Financial Self-Determinism and Control
The cryptocurrency networks are one of a kind because they are a digital store of value where people can securely save cryptocurrency units and enter into transactions without the need to rely on any third party regulatory body. After you have acquired and safely secured your cryptocurrency units, it is almost impossible for other people (thieves, hackers, banks or even the government) to take them away from you. The government cannot authorize the freezing of your cryptocurrency account nor stop you from entering into any transactions within the cryptocurrency network. This is the primary reason why people love cryptocurrencies, because the lack of regulation allows free movement of money. The government can only

do as much as track cryptocurrency purchases with fiat currencies but they cannot track purchases using cryptocurrencies by the individual.

Lower Cost of Transactions

While frozen accounts may be problematic, you also need to be aware of the cost of getting a transaction ready for use. On top of the unexpected risks of frozen accounts and massive chargebacks, when you use payment processors you will also be exposed to well-known high transaction charges for the services of these payment processors. This can considerably reduce the income of your business.

The transaction charges of PayPal, Google Checkout and Amazon Checkout all begin at 2.9 percent plus $ 0.30 for each transaction. You can enjoy a lower rate of 1.9 percent only if your total transactions for the month amount to more than $ 30,000. Because of this, these exorbitant fees may burden a business with a low-profit margin. The same goes for businesses that require a lot of smaller transactions or those whose products are sold at a nominal price.

In contrast to current day transactions, cryptocurrencies are known for their low fees, a major reason why banks are looking to adopt them. The fees vary according to which cryptocurrency is being traded. Bitcoin is known for their high fees relative to other cryptocurrencies; however, Ethereum and Litecoin can have fees less than 1%. And then there is Ripple... It is basically free (not free but it's really cheap) to send Ripple tokens around.

The cryptocurrency network is considered to be an intrinsically wide-reaching and global network. One of the biggest arguments for cryptocurrencies is the fast and low-cost transaction speeds across the world. You will not have to pass through artificial barriers to make payments to vendors who are based in other countries or regions. It is not entirely possible to validate where a particular cryptocurrency transaction originated. An online vendor who accepts cryptocurrency units as a mode of payment can instantly gain access to a global market while facing the risk of non-payment from customers who reside outside his own country. For example, this will allow individuals from the United States to send money to people in Australia in less than 10 minutes, making this much more convenient than third party transactions which are costly. I tried sending money through Western Union and they charged me around 1.5% on top of a poor exchange rate. With cryptocurrencies, I can send some Litecoin in less than 5 minutes and it'll cost around 20 cents.

You should be aware of whether cryptocurrency use in your area is valid and viable for use. The legality of cryptocurrencies will vary based on the country you get your transaction in. In 2017, the cryptocurrency world saw a larger adoption in cryptocurrency use and technology. In fact, more Bitcoin ATMs are available, allowing withdrawal of Bitcoin to cash; more vendors are also accepting Bitcoin and other cryptocurrencies as a form of payments. These signs show the availability and potential of cryptocurrencies. That being said, there are also countries that are closing off cryptocurrencies.

Risks

Volatility of Cryptocurrency Prices

When someone asks you what the value of the cryptocurrency units that you own is, how can you readily answer the question? The fundamental value of any particular currency is a function of the consumer demand for that currency and the consumers' capability to use the currency to trade it for valuable goods and services. Because a lot of conventional currencies are no longer linked to the worth of an underlying product or commodity such as gold and other precious metals, a cryptocurrency unit will only be valuable when some people or consumers want to own them and use them for trade. So if one day the world decides there is no longer a need for cryptocurrencies, the prices will plummet. Though this is unlikely, it is still a potential risk. Currently, there are plenty (approximately 7000) of public exchanges that have been set up to allow consumers to buy and sell cryptocurrency units in exchange for dollars or other common currencies. This aids in establishing a fundamental relative value for cryptocurrencies, which then allow vendors to convert their cryptocurrency holdings into other common currencies on a more regular basis. This minimizes the vendors' risk exposure to the price volatility of cryptocurrencies. As more individuals trade cryptocurrencies, the likely hood of cryptocurrencies to become more adopted increases.

Even though during the recent years, the price of cryptocurrencies has significantly fluctuated, there now exist methods that vendors can use to quote cryptocurrency prices relative to their equivalent value in dollar or other common currency. This also allows them to convert the cryptocurrencies they have collected into another currency immediately. A common database for cryptocurrency prices is www.coinmarketcap.com, which shows all cryptocurrencies available on the market, all historical prices, all exchanges with everything you need to know.

This comparatively small market limitation together with the absence of a regulatory body may expose the prices of cryptocurrencies to become manipulated by the market players. It's like what you would expect out of penny stocks and other items that are not as commonplace; it only takes one or two transactions for the values of certain items to be jacked up and artificially influenced. In the past, when there has been positive news, or speculation, some institutions (even countries) can jack up the prices. This has been seen frequently with the Korean market, jacking up various cryptocurrencies such as Ethereum, Ripple and Litecoin (amongst many), resulting in periods where 50% of trade occurs solely in the Korean market.

Several important speculations are being made in various online forums on who may be behind the price manipulation of cryptocurrencies and to what extent. It is quite common to hear cryptocurrency speculators refer to "The

Manipulator" when they discuss significant market movements.

"The Manipulator" refers to an unidentified individual or group of people that are assumed to be controlling the cryptocurrency prices through their vast wealth. But it is not clear as to who these people are.

There are various social media channels and networks such as Facebook groups, Youtube channels and other sites such as Reddit, that contain a lot of hype by individuals with extensive influence. Keep in mind, even though they might have a rational reason for their 'hyping' of a specified coin, this could also be considered as market manipulation. My advice is not to take my advice, but also do your own research. There are plenty of individuals that are invested in specific coins that only want to make money. Know what you're investing in. Period.

One thing is for certain that the relatively anonymous nature of cryptocurrencies is a huge part of what allows people to adjust the values of cryptocurrencies as they see fit. This makes for an added risk to the cryptocurrency. Of course, whoever is regulating it could always stop doing so and focus on some other kind of investment in the future, but it can be near impossible to figure out what's going to happen.

Risk of Loss

When you own cryptocurrency units, it is quite apparent that you have the responsibility to ensure that your digital wallet is secured from any potential hazards of loss and theft. This task or responsibility can be quite taxing, especially if you own a substantial number of cryptocurrencies because you will have to use certain tools such as protected encryption, password management and information backup to make sure that your risks are maintained at a low-level.

Several high-profile incidents have already been reported where people made errors and mistakes in handling their cryptocurrency accounts that ultimately led to them losing a large amount of their cryptocurrencies. Since there is no central authority you can approach to seek help or assistance, you may have to completely write off your losses because they may already be unrecoverable.

The risks associated with cryptocurrencies are critical and have to be identified. It should not be a surprise that a virtual currency that is relatively new is in danger of being hacked into. You should be cautious when seeing how this currency is run before you make any trades with it.

Few things to consider...
• Although it may seem common sense, NEVER-hand out your private keys to anyone. The private keys given by any wallet is the code that allows direct access to your cryptocurrencies.
• Consider a hardware device. Keeping your funds offline can be added protection, however, the risk of losing your hard-wallet is likely.
• Never leave funds on exchanges. If you've been in the cryptocurrency world for a while, you would know several major hacks in the past

that has resulted in multi-million dollar loses. Most notably the Mt. Gox hack.

Additionally, leaving your cryptocurrencies on exchanges leaves your funds subject to the exchanges' rules. A good example is the incident on 1st August 2017, with the introduction of Bitcoin Cash. Any Bitcoin owned on Coinbase, is subject to Coinbase' terms and conditions. Coinbase chose not to give any Bitcoin Cash to any Bitcoin owners during the Bitcoin hardfork. Exchanges are not liable for any loss that has occurred, so protect yourself.

Regulatory Ambiguity
The legal category of cryptocurrencies remains uncertain. Some people consider it as a commodity like gold and silver while other treat it as a viable currency. Still, there are others who look at them as a financial product or something that is legally equal to the gold in World of Warcraft. It is yet to be known if they will someday require licenses and financial rules

and regulations for it to become a truly viable currency.

Mt.Gox, which was considered as the biggest Bitcoin exchange market, has reported that they have experienced some difficulties in wiring funds. This is because of certain money laundering investigations done by the government or regulatory agencies.

But cryptocurrencies are intrinsically difficult to regulate because no central authority oversees all transactions. Because of this, it is highly probable that cryptocurrencies can become the primary medium option for people who are into illicit activities such as money laundering and tax evasion.

What makes the cryptocurrency market such a concern is that the protected nature of the currency makes it popular among those who engage in illegal or questionable activities.

But if we stop and think about it, any paper currency such as the US dollar can also have the same risks as described above. It is also possible to complete illegal transactions anonymously using dollar bills because it is possible to exchange it without any auditable paper trails. But the complexity of the cryptocurrency network technology may instigate regulators to see it as a hazard to the rules of law.

Chapter 5: Tips For Trading

Cryptocurrencies are also known as virtual currencies, and their share in the fiscal economy is rapidly increasing. As of now, there are more than 800 cryptocurrencies. Investing in cryptos isn't an exact rocket science. Unlike a company that publicly trades its stocks, there are no financial statements to go through or compare and therefore it is impossible to calculate their book value. Since the intrinsic value of cryptos isn't known, it is difficult to determine whether they have been undervalued or not.

A simple trading fact that you should accept is that you will never be able to time your buys or sells correctly in the crypto space. Selling isn't an exact science and, therefore, there isn't one single strategy that you can follow to acquire more wealth. Every trader has different goals, and all cryptocurrencies are different. No two traders or currencies are alike. In this section, you will learn about some tips that you can make use of while investing in cryptocurrencies.

Understanding the power of cryptocurrencies

People tend to think that investing in cryptocurrencies is the same as investing in stocks. Well, cryptocurrencies aren't stocks, and they aren't commodities. Cryptocurrencies have prices but are entirely different from stocks fundamentally. The process of exchange might be similar. The underlying technology that powers different cryptos can be potentially adapted for retail and institutional capital. The decentralized nature of the digitized currencies means that there isn't much scope for their manipulation. You should invest in cryptos because that's the future of investments and you should believe in it as well.

Select a strategy

How often do you want to buy or sell? Do you want to be a day trader, or do you want to hold on to your cryptos for a while? The general rule of thumb is that the longer you hold your digitized tokens for, the less is the risk you can incur. The same rule of investing that applies to stocks applies to cryptocurrencies as well. However, this doesn't mean that when the circumstances aren't favorable, you hold on to them. Learn to cut your losses and exit when it seems like you are losing in the market. Structural issues are an indicator of failure and learn to recognize such signs.

The initial investment

Dollar cost averaging your purchases of cryptocurrencies will help in reducing the risk of any sudden changes. This will help to reduce the prick of any sudden price fluctuations the tokens might experience in the market. Stick to your gut when it comes to investing, but this doesn't mean that you ignore the market trends.

Hedging your bets

Several exchanges allow you short orders as well. It allows you to place a bet on either side of the price movements of your cryptocurrencies. For instance, a simple strategy would be to put

90% on long and the rest on short orders. This approach means that you are confident about the extended position and it can be made use of for any level of risk.

Trading in altcoins

Bitcoins and other established cryptocurrencies might seem quite tempting. But the world of digitized currencies isn't restricted to just the popular cryptos. So, don't ignore other altcoins. The smaller market capitalization they offer means that they are prone to higher movements in their price. Different altcoins are created to cater to different needs and niches. The risk of investing in altcoins might be high, but then so are the returns. You can allocate specific percentages to different altcoins depending on your tolerance of risk. It is quite similar to managing a fund. Some altcoins are more stable than Ethereum, but others can be very volatile. So, a significant chunk of your portfolio can consist of the famous cryptocurrencies, and the rest can be made up of other altcoins.

Get into the game

Bitcoins are at an all-time high, and the returns they are offering are quite high as well. All the tips and information you have gathered so far will be of no use if you don't get into the game. You should get started with investing. After all, gaining experience is the best way to learn. Start with a small investment, and you can slowly progress towards more significant investments.

Separate wallets

Never use a single portfolio for storing all your cryptocurrencies. If you are using one wallet for spending and storing your cryptos, you are making yourself vulnerable to cyber threats and attacks. You can create as many Bitcoin addresses as you want. So, it makes sense to make use of different wallets for this purpose. Use different addresses for storing, sending, and receiving cryptocurrencies.

Web wallets shouldn't be used for safekeeping

Web wallets are easy to use. However, it doesn't necessarily mean that they are secure as well. In fact, you are making yourself a soft target for all the potential hackers. If someone manages to hack into your web wallet, you might as well forget about your precious coins. You can make use of a web wallet to hold onto small savings and quick transactions, but that's about it. Always store your savings on a hardware wallet that isn't online. Cryptos don't work for your credit or debit cards. Once your card gets stolen, you lose it or even forget the password; you have the option of blocking and receiving a new one. However, you cannot do this with cryptocurrencies. Since the network is based on anonymity and it is decentralized, there isn't a regulatory authority that you can report the theft too, and you are bound to lose your coins. So, be careful with your tokens.

Protecting your privacy

You are the only one who is responsible for your security and no one else. You wouldn't share the

PIN of your bank account with others, would you? Similarly, you shouldn't share your private key with anyone else. The wallet address you use is like your bank account, and your key is like the PIN. The private key is necessary to officiate a transaction. Anyone who is in possession of your private key and the wallet address can easily siphon the funds from your account. Let us keep all the technical aspects aside for a moment. Isn't it foolish to divulge your private information to a stranger?

Cold storage

You are vulnerable, even if your cryptocurrency is stored in a wallet on your computer. Applications of different wallets tend to store user data, and its location can be predicted easily. It is a severe breach of security if someone can access all your financial information. A simple solution is to store your private key on an offline media. Ensuring additional safety will do you no harm, and it will help in securing your hard-earned money. You have the option of printing the private key on a piece of paper or even store it on a USB. You can scan your QR code and save it. Another option is the encryption of your key. Without the code to decrypt it, the numbers of the key would be useless.

Back it up

Now that you have secured your cryptocurrencies from others, the next step is to protect it from yourself. Yes, you need to protect it from yourself as well. Always make it a point to back up your wallet. Scan your private key and store it in a couple of places. Make multiple copies so that even if one copy is lost, you can still retrieve your secret key without worrying about preceding your investment.

Never invest more than you can afford to lose
When it comes to investing in any form of security, it is essential that you spend wisely. You should never invest more than the loss you can afford. Cryptos are volatile and speculative.

The chances of earning a profit or incurring a loss are equally high. So, if you are taking a risk, make sure that it is a calculated one and not an impulsive one. One poor decision can lead to a significant loss. You should be comfortable with the investment that you are making. Always prepare for the worst, you never know what might happen to your investment. You might even end up losing everything. Also, try and diversify your portfolio so that you don't miss everything due to the volatility of a single cryptocurrency.

Set goals for every trade you make

It is quintessential that you have set goals for every deal that you think of making. It will help to keep a steady mind even when the market conditions aren't favorable. Set a price limit at which you should take profits and cut your losses. Set these two limits before you think about entering the market. This will help you in staying level headed without getting swayed by emotions.

Technology

If you are thinking about investing in a programmable currency then you will need a basic understanding of the underlying technology. Most cryptocurrencies make use of the same code as that of a Bitcoin and are just pale copies of the former. Therefore, the investor tends to take little interest in it, unless the Bitcoin fails, as another cryptocurrency can act as its substitute. Take into consideration the validation system that the blockchain makes use of. Does the cryptocurrency make the method of proof of work or evidence of stake? Both are being used simultaneously, or neither is being used. Does it use any other algorithm to check the transactions on the blockchain? What's the governance that's involved, if any? What method of scalability is considered? Is the cryptocurrency even making use of a blockchain? Cryptocurrencies that don't possess the same characteristics as the Bitcoin or the ones that don't use the same language for programming should be studied carefully. Don't assume that all the cryptocurrencies are the same.

The number of tokens created

As an investor, you will be buying tokens, so you should check if the cryptocurrency has a finite number of tokens and if the system is deflationary. The quantum of coins in existence can increase or decrease the price of the cryptocurrency at any point in time. For instance, Bitcoin and Bitcoin cash can only have 21 million tokens at any point in time. So, this is a scarce resource, and with an increase in their demand, their value is bound to increase as well.

The price of a token

Finding a virtual currency that seems to be promising isn't sufficient, you should also know when to buy it. A cryptocurrency can be purchased before its official launch by participating in an ICO or Initial Coin Offering. However, you need to take into consideration the fact that the price of the currency can drop significantly after the brief high of an ICO. If you have missed the ICO, then don't worry. Just wait until the public attention fades away. The price of a cryptocurrency is bound to increase when it is added to an existing trading platform, is taken up by a famous wallet service or when it has reached the stage of track record. It is wise to buy these tokens before the happening of any of these events when the price isn't too high, and you still have a safety margin working in your favor. There are different trading platforms, websites, and exchanges that will provide you with the necessary charts for judging the performance of a cryptocurrency.

Website matters

Check whether the cryptocurrency you want to invest in has an official website of its own. Is there any information available about its creators or the company that's running the operations? Are there any developers and, if yes, then are there biographies and any white papers describing the nature of the cryptocurrency in question? If you cannot find all this information, then it is better if you stay away from such currency. What if it turns out to be a Ponzi scam? Don't invest blindly.

Slack

Slack is the communication platform used by most of the cryptocurrency developers. By registering yourself on slack, you can obtain all the necessary information about the performance of the cryptocurrencies and any advancement made in this regard. Always take into consideration the developers who are responsible for the creation of a particular token. So, do plenty of research, read about the team, and acquire all the information needed and only then should you make a decision about investing. Being prudent is quintessential.

Mistakes to avoid

There are a couple of errors that you should avoid if you want to invest in cryptocurrencies successfully. The first thing that you should do is store your crypto offline. Security should be your priority, and you should always secure your digitized currencies. Once they are lost, they cannot be recovered. Take precautions while storing your cryptos and store them offline. Don't forget that if you don't have your private key, you cannot access your coins. Do not get carried away by any pump and dump groups. Don't follow these teams and don't think of a quick buy. Instead, do your research and invest in coins sensibly. When in doubt, invest in the popular coins before you think about the obscure ones. Most people tend to buy or spend in certain cryptos because they are considered to be a hot investment at present. However, don't do this. Investing in a crypto that you know nothing about will do you no good. So, take some time and do plenty of research before jumping into the market. Who wouldn't want to make a quick buck? ICOs tend to promote this, but that doesn't mean they are an excellent investing option. Like with any other form of investment, you should do plenty of research on your own before investing in an ICO. After all, it is your hard-earned money that you are thinking about investing. So, that is the least you can do. Don't panic and sell your position. You will end up regretting it. Don't let your emotions guide you when you are engaging in a trade. Be practical and only take calculated risks. Never seek advice from a stranger. Do your research and trust your channels. Make a decision just after gaining a thorough understanding of the crypto you have opted for.

Chapter 6: The Most Common Cryptocurrencies

An inspection of coinmarketcap or one of the other sites showing cryptocurrencies reveals a great many other cryptocurrencies than Bitcoin and Ethereum. These won't all be discussed, however, in the top ten near the middle of November 2017, I found Bitcoin, Ethereum, Bitcoin Cash, Ripple, Litecoin, Dash, Monero, Neo, NEM, Ethereum Classic as the top ten then IOTA. I mention IOTA, as it is a particularly interesting cryptocurrency.

Bitcoin Cash(BCH): On August 1st, 2017, there was, what is called in the cryptocurrency world, a soft fork on the Bitcoin Network. This led to a brand new cryptocurrency, Bitcoin Cash (BCC), often BCC is written as BCH. This new currency arose because of major differences in the community of Bitcoin.

The problems leading to this have never been completely resolved and consequently, there was to be what is called a hard fork on the Bitcoin blockchain, called the SegWit2. This hard fork never took place.

In the August 2017 soft fork, anyone in possession of the old coin received the same value of the new coin. There were many who did not want the new coin and attempted to sell them immediately. Whether this was possible, depended on the exchanges they used. There were some exchanges that would not trade in Bitcoin Cash.

Some well-known exchanges such as Bittrex, Kraken, CoinOne, Coinbase , and Poloniex did trade in it and since August 2017, Bitcoin Cash has gone from strength to strength, on November 17, one BCH was worth $1,369, over a 100% increase in one week.

What is all this fork stuff anyway? It concerns the blocks of the blockchain, the tables containing information about transactions. One Bitcoin (BTC) has 1Mb, maximum block size, and as a result only 250,000 transactions BTC per day are possible, with 7 transactions per second. Bitcoin Cash(BCC) has a maximum 8Mb block size limit that allows many more transactions per second.

The number of transactions, with this could be about 2,000,000 per day. When you consider that the VISA system is capable of handling up to 56,000 transactions per second, with an average of about 2,000 and daily peak of about 4,000, you see there is a big problem. A problem of scalability that Bitcoin must solve if it is to replace fiat money.

Not withstanding the difference in blocksize, there are not many differences in how you can use the two coins are used.

Ripple: On November 13 2017, Ripple (XRP) was the fourth most valuable cryptocurrency. It is not possible to mine Ripple, as you can mine

Bitcoin or Ether. In the cryptoworld, Ripple is almost an old timer, as it started in 2012. Ripple is open source, it is not owned by a company such as Microsoft with Office or Adobe with Photoshop.

Ripple resembles Bitcoin, as its network enables P2P trading and transactions need approval by a distributed network of computers. Mining does this for Bitcoin and Ether. The method Ripple uses is iterative consensus and this is different to mining. Reasons for this difference are extremely technical; they explain why you cannot mine Ripple. Iterative consensus allows for transactions that are far quicker and more energy efficient.

There was a proposal to build an XRP network for the creation of smart contracts. This was to be called codius. Codius has not gained nearly the same popularity, for this purpose, as Ethereum. Ripple is mainly used for financial settlements. Japan, the third largest economy in the world, accepts Ripple as currency.

Earlier we stated that the number of Bitcoin would never exceed 21,000,000. Similarly, the number of Ripple has a maximum of 100,000,000,000.

Dash(DASH): A cryptocurrency, highly rated as regards privacy and anonymity is Dash. One of the reasons for this is that Dash has fungibility.

What is fungibility? A coin has fungibility if a unit of the currency is of equal value in A as in B, its value is independent of location.

One of the reasons for the enhanced privacy and anonymity is that Dash possesses something called PrivateSend, which mixes Dash coins anonymously over different points in its network. There is a feature on PrivateSend that gives Dash less appeal to criminals, and PrivateSend helps maintain fungibility. Fungibility is even better than encryption at maintaining both anonymity and value.

On Nov 13 2017, Dash had capitalization in excess of $4 billion and was ranked about 5th.

One DASH exceeded $500 (US), which is more than a doubling of value in two months. It is wrong to confuse Dash with either CoinDash(CDT) or Dashcoin(DSH), which are totally different coins.

Litecoin: Litecoin (LTC) is a child of Bitcoin. On November 13, 2017, Litecoin had market capitalization of more than $3 billion (US) and one Litecoin had a value of $59 (US). It was created by a man called Charlie Lee, who used to work for Google. There can never be more than 84 million LTC. It is quite similar to Bitcoin, but has more features. It is interesting to note that Litecoin has SegWit activated, while Bitcoin just repudiated SegWit. Litecoin is quicker than Bitcoin; Litecoin blocks are produced about four times as frequently as Bitcoin, however, Litecoin is not as secure as Bitcoin. If privacy is an issue then Litecoin is no more private than Bitcoin.

Monero (XMR): Monero is another favorite of those seeking an anonymity-oriented alt coin. Monero began in 2014 and on November 13

2017, was number 7 by market capitalization of cryptocurrencies, with capitalization of nearly $2 billion (US) and 1 XMR worth more than $125 (US). Monero has always put a high premium on very high levels of privacy. In spite of that, a report in 2017 described a serious problem in Monero code; this has been rectified.

NEO(NEO): Neo is a crypto currency, originally called AntShares is, created in China. It has been created to be in sync with Chinese government rulings on cryptocurrency. Like Ethereum, NEO is a platform, which enables the development of smart contracts. NEO has collaborated with Microsoft to create some of its features. The problem of scalability has been taken very seriously and NEO claims to be able to handle 1000 transactions per second and eventually 10,000! This compares very favorably with Bitcoin's 7 transactions per second, and Ethereum's 15 transactions per second. A particularly useful feature of NEO is NeoFS, which involves the storage of large files on nodes in the NEO network. Security has been taken very seriously and it is believed that even quantum computers, when they become common, will be unable to crack the security of the Neo network. NEO is a cryptocurrency with a market capitalization of more $1.75 billion (US), the value of one NEO is more than $20.

NEM(XEM): NEM (XEM), originated from Japan in 2015. Although cryptocurrency is opposed to banks, Japanese banks have assisted the development of NEM. NEM has a consensus mechanism called proof- of -importance rather than the proof-of-stake, which is typical of other crypto currencies. NEM was written using the Java computer language. NEM has inbuilt features that discourage wealth inequality and encourage transactions on the networks. These features have not been addressed, to any large degree, by other crypto currencies. NEM is a cryptocurrency with a market capitalization of more $1.65 billion (US), the value of one XEM is only $0.2.

Ethereum Classic(ETC): Ethereum Classic rounded out the top ten cryptocurrencies, when I checked on the coinmarketcap site in mid November 2017. As with Bitcoin Cash, Ethereum Classic (ETC), a cryptocurrency with a market capitalization of more $1.5 billion (US), resulted from a fork, although this took place on the Ethereum blockchain and not the Bitcoin blockchain. Far more could be said about this however it is sufficient to state that the value of one Ethereum Classic coin was worth more than $15 (US) in mid November 2017.

IOTA (MIOTA): IOTA is very interesting cryptocurrency. It has been specifically created for the Internet of Things (IoT). You could well say,"What is the IoT?" The Internet of Things is the Internet of Everything and involves lighting, infrastructure, gas and just about any appliance. As the IoT becomes a reality then the Internet will feature in all parts of our lives.

Unlike many other cryptocurrencies such as Bitcoin and Ethereum, IOTA does not use a blockchain. In contrast to blockchain, IOTA has no blocks; it uses the Tangle. The Tangle is a very interesting system with a new way of reaching consensus. The Tangle is known as a directed acyclic graph (DAG) in mathematics and computer science. The Tangle is the distributed ledger, stored on the nodes of the network of IOTA. The Tangle will permit the scalability, so very lacking from Bitcoin and Ethereum.

A very interesting facet of IOTA is that it provides protection if there is quantum-computing. Quantum computing is founded on the idea that rather than having only 2 states 0 and 1, there are three states. If quantum computing becomes a reality, then many current encryption systems will be at risk. IOTA, like NEO, has worked to overcome this danger, before it arises. You may recall that this was a feature of the cryptocurrency NEO.

IOTA has a market capitalization of more $1.65 billion (US), the value of one MIOTA is only $0.60.

In addition to these top cryptocurrencies, there are literally hundreds of others. Have a look at the site of coinmarketcap to see many of them.

Chapter 7: Cryptocurrency Exchanges

What does a cryptocurrency exchange mean? There are certain cryptocurrency websites where you can sell, purchase or trade cryptocurrencies for any other form of digital or traditional currency. These sites are referred to as cryptocurrency exchanges. For those who are interested in trading professionally and want access to trading tools, then they will need a cryptocurrency exchange that requires an ID and an account for operating. If you are interested in trading occasionally or casually, then there are platforms that you can make use of without creating a trading account.

Types of exchanges
There are a couple of types of exchanges that you can make use of like-
Trading platforms

All the websites that connect different buyers and sellers. These websites charge a fee on every transaction that takes place.

Direct trading

These websites are designed to offer a direct person-to-person trading platform where individuals from anywhere in the world can gather to exchange currencies. Direct trading exchanges don't have a market price, and instead, each seller has the option of setting their exchange rate.

Brokers

These are the websites that anyone interested in buying cryptocurrencies can visit, and buy the currency at a listed price. Cryptocurrency brokers are quite similar to the dealers of foreign exchange.

Things to consider

Before you think about trading, there are a couple of things that you need to take into consideration. You should do your homework about the following things before you make your first trade.

Reputation:

The best way to gather information about a particular exchange is to search about it from the reviews given by individual users and also well-known websites providing information about the industry. You can enquire about it on other platforms and forums like Reddit or BitcoinTalk. Refer to financial and economic magazines and blogs for gathering all the necessary information.

Fees:

Most of the exchanges do provide information about the chargeable fees on a transaction, and you should be able to find this on the related website. Before joining a platform, make sure that you understand their policies regarding deposits, transactions, and even withdrawal fees. Depending on the exchange and your usage, the fees can vary substantially.

Mode of payment:

Understand the different modes of payment that are provided by the exchange. Maybe they use credit cards, debit cards, wire transfers, or even PayPal. If an exchange has restricted or limited payment options, then it might not be the most convenient option available for you. Whenever you want to purchase any cryptocurrency with your credit card, then you will need to verify your identity, and this also comes with a higher transaction and processing fees. Also, the risk of fraud is higher too. Acquiring cryptocurrency through a wire transfer can take a while since it needs to be processed and verified by the concerned bank first.

Verification:

Most of the trading platforms located in the US and UK require some form of ID proof for making deposits and withdrawals. There are some that provide anonymity. The process of verification can take up to a couple of days, and it might seem a little troublesome. But it is in your interest, and it helps in protecting the exchange from the possibility of theft, fraud, and other scams.

Geographical restrictions:

There are a few user-specific functions like an exchange offer, which is accessible only in certain countries. Make sure that the exchange you are opting for provides complete access to all tools and functions regardless of the country you are located in.

Exchange rate:

Different exchanges have different exchange rates. You will probably be surprised about the amount that you can save by doing a little bit of research. At times, the exchange rates can go up to 10% or even higher. So, do your research carefully.

Best cryptocurrency exchanges

There are plenty of platforms, and they all aren't created equally. The list of platforms mentioned below includes some of the most popular cryptocurrency exchanges regarding user-friendliness, fees charged, accessibility, and the security offered. Here is the list of the best exchanges in no particular order.

Coinbase:

This is widely trusted by several investors and is used by millions of individuals globally. Coinbase is amongst the most popular crypto exchanges, famous brokers, and well-known trading platforms in the world at the moment. Coinbase makes it easy for securely buying, using, storing, and trading digitized currency. Users can cryptocurrencies like Bitcoins, Litecoins, and Ethereum by using this website through a digital wallet that is available for devices supported by android and iOS. They can also trade with other users by using the Global Digital Asset Exchange or GDAX subsidiary of Coinbase. GDAX is currently operation in the US, UK, Europe, Canada, Australia, and Singapore. There is no exchange fee that is chargeable by GDAX currently for transferring funder between the Coinbase and GDAX accounts. For now, depending on the country you reside in, the selection of tradable currencies will vary. You can head to their website to learn more about this platform.

This platform has a good reputation, offers security, the transactional cost is reasonable, the interface is user-friendly, and the currency that's stored in Coinbase is covered by its insurance. However, on the flipside, the customer support needs to improve, the payment options are limited, it is available in only a limited number of countries, the rollout of services isn't uniform, and GDAX is apt for technical traders.

Kraken:

It was founded in the year 2011, and it is the largest Bitcoin exchange platform in the euro volume traded and liquidity offered. It is a partner in the first cryptocurrency bank created as well. Kraken allows its users to buy and sell Bitcoins and trade Bitcoins in exchange for euros, US dollars, Canadian dollars, British pounds, and the Japanese yen. The other cryptocurrencies that can be traded on this platform include Ethereum or ether, Monero, Augur REP tokens, Ripple, ICONOMI, Litecoin, Zcash, Dogecoin, and Lumens. For the experienced users, Kraken also offers margin trading other advanced trading features. Check the official website of Kraken for gaining better insight.

This platform boasts of good reputation, reasonable fair exchange rates, the cost of transactions is low, the deposit fee is minimal, offers plenty of features, provides good customer support, very secure, and is supported all over the world. On the downside, the payment options are limited, it is not the best platform for beginners, and the user interface isn't intuitive.

Cex.io:
This platform provides a host of services for the users of Bitcoins and other cryptocurrencies. It allows its users to easily trade their fiat currency for cryptocurrencies and the other way around as well. If you are looking for a platform that will allow the users to trade in Bitcoins professionally, then Cex.io offers several personalized trading dashboards that are user-friendly and provides the option of margin trading as well. Not just that, but it provides novice traders with a really simple way of buying Bitcoins at a price that is almost the same as the market rate. This website is secure, and the

cryptocurrencies can be stored in the safe for cold storage.

This platform enjoys a good reputation, it supports credit cards, a good mobile application, and good for beginners, the exchange rates are decent, and it provides worldwide support. However, the customer support is just about average, the process of verification is lengthy, and depositing is quite expensive.

ShapeShift:

This is one of the leading exchanged, and it supports different types of cryptocurrencies like Bitcoin, ether, Monero, Zcash, dash, Dogecoin, and many others as well. This is an excellent option for anyone who is interested in conducting straightforward trades without having to sign up, creating a platform or having to depend on a platform for the safekeeping of their funds. This platform doesn't allow a user to purchase cryptocurrency by making use of credit or debit cards. The platform has a strict no fiat money policy and is solely for the exchange of one cryptocurrency for another cryptocurrency. Please do visit their official website to learn more about their trading policies.

This trading platform has a good reputation in the market, is beginner friendly, the prices are reasonable, the time for processing a transaction is less, and it offers plenty of cryptocurrencies. On the down side, their mobile application isn't that great; it doesn't allow any fiat currencies, the payment options are limited, and provides only a few tools.

Poloniex:

It is one of the most popular cryptocurrency exchanges, and it was founded in the year 2014. The transaction provides a secured trading platform with over 100 Bitcoin-cryptocurrency pairings and several advanced tools and data analysis as well. This trading platform has one of the highest trading volumes recorded, and the users always have the option of closing their trade position. It uses a volume-tiered and a maker-taker schedule for fees for all the trades. So, the fee payable will be different depending on whether you are a maker or a taker. For makers, the fee can range anywhere from 0-0.15% depending on the quantum of trade conducted. Whereas for takers, the fee can range from 0.10-0.25%. There is no fee levied on withdrawals that go beyond the transaction fee needed by the network. The chat box offered by this platform is one of its unique features, and this allows the user to obtain help about anything related to cryptocurrencies. Any user is allowed to write what they want, and if the comment is inappropriate, then the moderator can take it down. At times it isn't easy to distinguish between good and bad advice, but the chat box is a great tool to increase user engagement.

The creation of an account on this platform isn't time-consuming, there are plenty of useful features, BTC lending is facilitated, the volume of trading is high, easy to use, the trading fee is low, and it has an open API. However, the customer support service is slow, and it doesn't support fiat currencies.

Bitstamp:

This is a European Union Bitcoin marketplace that was created in 2011. This platform is amongst the first-gen Bitcoin exchanges that have managed to develop a loyal customer base for itself. It is a well-known and quite trusted throughout the Bitcoin community and is a very safe platform. It offers several security features like the two-step authentication procedure and the multi-signature technology for its cryptocurrency wallet and has a cold storage that is fully insured. It offers 24/7 customer support to its users, and the user interface is multilingual. Starting or creating your account is quite easy. Once you have opened a free account and have made a deposit, then the users are free to start trading as soon as they want to.

This platform enjoys a good reputation, provides high-level security to its users, has worldwide availability, the transaction fee is low, and it is best suited for large transactions. It isn't as user-friendly as other platforms, there are only a couple of payment options it offers, and the deposit fee is high.

CoinMama:

This is a veteran broker exchange, and anyone can visit it for buying Bitcoin or Ethereum by making use of credit cards or cash via MoneyGram or the Western Union. This was created for those who would like to make an instant or a straightforward purchase of digital currency by using the local fiat currency. This service is available to users all over the world, but there are some countries where the users might not be able to access all the functions provided by this website. The user interface is available in several languages like English, German, French, Russian, and Italian as well.

This is a great platform for users, and it enjoys a good reputation. The user interface is good, it offers different payment options, worldwide availability, and the transaction time is relatively good. However, the exchange rates are high; a premium fee is chargeable on credit cards, no Bitcoin selling function and the customer service is just about average.

Bitsquare:

This is an easy-to-use and user-friendly peer-to-peer exchange that allows the users to buy and sell their Bitcoins in exchange for other cryptocurrencies or even fiat currencies. It markets itself a decentralized peer-to-peer platform and is accessible instantly and doesn't need any registration and indeed doesn't depend on a central authority. This platform never holds onto the funds of the user expect the trading partners who an exchange their data. The platform provides good security coupled with MultiSigna addresses, a security deposit, and a self-built arbitration system for solving any trading disputes. If anonymity is a high priority for you, then this is a wonderful platform for you.

It enjoys an excellent reputation in the market; it is quite secure and private, a lot of cryptocurrency options are available, it doesn't require the user to sign up for it, it is an open source with worldwide availability, and is best suited for advanced traders. But the payment options offered are limited, the customer support can be better, and it isn't the best place for first-time traders.

LocalBitcoin:

This is a peer-to-peer Bitcoin exchange, and the buyers and sellers are located all over the world. By using this platform, you have the option of meeting up with others in your surroundings for trading in Bitcoins for cash, sending money through PayPal, Skrill, or Dwolla, or even arrange for the required amount to be deposited at a bank branch. The commission chargeable from sellers is 1%, and the sellers are allowed to set their exchange rates. For making sure that the trade is secure, this platform takes plenty of precautions. This platform always rates the traders transacting on it, and this information is public. Also, whenever a trade is requested, then this platform holds those funds in its escrow account and only when the seller confirms the trade will these funds be released. If something goes wrong, it has its team for resolution of conflicts and disputes between sellers and buyers.

This platform doesn't need an ID, it is user and beginner friendly, it usually is free, the transfers are instant, and it is available all over the world. However, the exchange rates are high, and it doesn't facilitate large purchases of Bitcoins.

Gemini:
This platform was co-founded by Tyler Winklevoss and Cameron Winklevoss. It is a fully regulated and licensed US exchange of Bitcoin and ether. This means that the capital requirements, as well as its regulatory standards, should be similar to a bank. Also, if a deposit is made in US dollars then the same would be held in a bank insured by FDIC and most of the digital currency held on it is in cold storage. It trades in only three currencies, and

these are US dollar, Bitcoin, and Ethereum. It doesn't serve any other form of crypto or fiat currencies. The exchange has a maker-taker fee schedule with discounts for a trade of high volume. There is no charge on all the deposits and withdrawals. It is entirely available to its customers in 42 US states, Canada, Hong Kong, Japan, Singapore, South Korea and the UK.

The security and compliance offered are exceptional, it is minimalistic and elegant in its design, is user-friendly, provides excellent analytics, and ensures high liquidity. However, the number of currencies offered is limited, has a small community, doesn't have worldwide availability, and doesn't offer margin trading.

If you are thinking about making your first trade, then make sure that you have plenty of research about the trading platform you are opting for.

Chapter 8: The Future Of Cryptocurrency

While the relatively short amount of time cryptocurrency has been around makes it difficult to chart its future, there are several different events taking place worldwide that give some clue, at least, into what the future of cryptocurrency could look like.

Increasing regulation: One of the key facets of Bitcoin at launch was the fact that it allowed for completely anonymous transactions to take place online. This, of course, led to countless illegal activities being perpetrated on the system, many of them, even now, centered around the Silk Road marketplace. Since this was first made known to the Department of Homeland Security, the SEC, FCN and the FBI, they have been working on a case that may be close to finally changing the status quo of Bitcoin forever.

At the same time, the Federal Reserve is currently working on another solution to the same problem. In this instance, they would cut off the Bitcoin problem at the source by simply releasing its own cryptocurrency instead. It is tentatively called Fedcoin and sources near the Federal Reserve say that it is closer to reality than you might think. This is because all it would take is a simple fork of the Bitcoin blockchain, coupled with a new genesis block, to get the new cryptocurrency up and running.

Initially, Fedcoins would be easy to exchange for USD on a one to one basis, though eventually it will likely be able to find places to purchase fiat currency. The biggest difference between it and other cryptocurrencies is the fact that the Federal Reserve would, of course, retain control over the blockchain which would give them the ability to create or destroy blocks at will. They would also be able to see all of the details surrounding every transaction, making Bitcoin's anonymity a thing of the past.

First national cryptocurrency: Proving once again that they are at the forefront of everything having to do with Cryptocurrency, China recently announced that they are on the verge of releasing their very own cryptocurrency, having already successfully completed tests between their central bank and other financial services. While many of the details remain unclear, the information that is already available, points to a cryptocurrency whose blockchain can scale essentially as needed, regardless of the level of demand that is placed on the system. It is tentatively scheduled to come to market around the same time that the renminbi is released, though a precise timetable remains unclear.

This marks a major step, not just for China, but for the idea of national cryptocurrencies as a whole. It also shows just how committed China is to working through the inevitable technical and economic challenges. Regardless of how it all works out, it is undoubtedly going to have serious repercussions on the world financial system in more ways than one; not to mention showing the world just what a centralized currency can do.

It will also mark the first time that a digital currency has a value that is directly tied to a bank note which has the potential to decrease transaction costs associated with all types of transactions made with the currency. It will also mark the first time an estimated hundred million Chinese citizens will have easy access to banking services, adding a significant chunk of onlinesales to the mix as well.

The cryptocurrency will also give the Chinese government some means to control the growth of speculative cryptocurrency trading that has been going on in the country, essentially without any oversight whatsoever. It also will be interesting to see how having a local alternative will affect the Chinese appetite for bitcoins and ether. The new currency is also going to give the government previously unimagined access to financial data and the related habits of its citizens as the currency is designed to be easy to track. This should help to cut down on the corruption China is currently facing in its banking sector as well.

Policymakers have also shown an interest into the insights that having access to all of this data will provide when it comes to motivating the local economy. The digital addition will also automatically make the renminbi more of a going concern as anyone in the world will be able to easily acquire and spend it, without having to deal with traditional exchange fees.

Conclusion

Thank you for making it through to the end of Cryptocurrency: The Fundamental Guide to Cryptocurrency Investing For Beginner's. Let's hope it was informative and able to provide you with all of the tools you need to achieve your goals, whatever it is that they may be. Just because you've finished this book doesn't mean there is nothing left to learn on the topic, expanding your horizons is the only way to find the mastery you seek.

When it comes to keeping up with the latest and greatest that is going on in the cryptocurrency world, it is important to keep in mind that things change at a lightning pace. What this means is that you need to get in the habit of becoming a lifelong learner if you hope to find success when dealing with this emerging market. The moment that you decide to rest on your laurels is the moment you risk losing out on serious profits.

Beyond that, it is important to enter the world of cryptocurrency with the right mindset to ensure that you find the success that you seek. While you can certainly blunder your way through a few trades and end up a millionaire, that is generally going to be the exception, not the rule. Instead, you are going to want to take a longer view and work on maximizing your profits as much as possible before mass saturation occurs, and the truly amazing profits will be gone forever.